THE BASICS OF MINISTRY SERIES

GUIDE FOR LECTORS

Aelred Rosser

LTP

LITURGY
TRAINING
PUBLICATIONS

ACKNOWLEDGMENTS

For a more extensive treatment of the ministry of the liturgical reader, see *A Well-Trained Tongue: Formation in the Ministry of Reader*, also by Aelred Rosser and available from Liturgy Training Publications. Much of what appears in this *Guide* is distilled from that larger work.

The lectionary texts contained herein are adapted from the *Lectionary of the Canadian Conference of Catholic Bishops*, copyright © Concacan, Inc., 1992, and are used by permission of the copyright owner. All rights reserved.

Martin F. Connell was the editor of this book. Deborah Bogaert was the production editor. Anna Manhart and Lisa Grayson designed it, and Kari Nicholls set the type in Goudy. Printed in the United States of America.

Cover photo by Antonio Perez. Photos on pages i, 19, 23 and 37 by Antonio Perez; photos on pages 1, 11, 27 and 48 by Bill Wittman; photo on page 6 by Gary Hannabarger.

GUIDE FOR LECTORS © 1998, 1999, 2002 Archdiocese of Chicago: Liturgy Training Publications, 1800 North Hermitage Avenue, Chicago IL 60622-1101; 1-800-933-1800; fax 1-800-933-7094; e-mail orders@ltp.org. All rights reserved.

Visit our website at www.ltp.org

05 04 03 02   6 5 4 3

Library of Congress Cataloging-in-Publication Data
Rosser, Aelred R. (Aelred Robert)
    Guide for lectors/ Aelred Rosser.
       p. c.m. — (Basics of ministry series)
    Includes bibliographical references.
    1. Lay readers — Catholic Church. I. Title. II. Series.
BX1915.R658   1998
264' .02034 — dc21   98-18222
                                                         CIP

    ISBN 1-56854-238-0
    EGLECT

Contents

The Lector's Ministry: Proclaiming the Good News

Making the Word Flesh . . . Again

"The word of the Lord." These five words tell us a lot about the ministry of the lector. Whether you are simply interested in liturgical ministry, are thinking about becoming a lector or have been serving in this ministry for a long time, think for a moment about the words "The word of the Lord."

When the proclaimer at the lectern finishes the reading, looks up at the assembly and says "The word of the Lord," something wonderful has happened. The mystery of God's interaction with us has been recalled, revived and renewed. That is, we have once again heard God reveal the divine intention to love, redeem and reclaim us. The promise, the covenant, that God has made with us has been written on our hearts again. The summons to return in obedience to the God from whom we have strayed through disobedience has been reissued. The unfathomable love God has for us, the love that God *is* for us, has been made flesh again.

All this has happened in the proclamation of God's word that we heard from the proclaimer's lips and in that little phrase that calls for our response: "The word of the Lord." "Thanks be to God," we answer. Thanks, indeed, to the God who summons us in love every time the word is proclaimed in our midst.

When we remind ourselves of all that is implied in "The word of the Lord," we have no difficulty understanding proclamation of the word as genuine ministry. The lector does what any good minister does: comforts us in our suffering, rouses us from our lethargy, confirms us in our faith, encourages us in our discouragement. All ministry is the noble and unselfish impulse to tell the good news of God's love for the world in Jesus Christ. To proclaim that good news from the sacred text is ministry *par excellence*. "When the scriptures are read in the church, it is Christ himself who speaks." So says the church in teaching us about liturgical prayer.

All Christians are, by definition, proclaimers of the good news. Because we were baptized into Christ's life, mission, death, resurrection and ascension, we announce to the world by our very existence that "Christ has died, Christ is risen, Christ will come again." Even as sinners — especially as repentant sinners — we proclaim the mercy of God and the truth of God's promise: "My word will not return to me void, but shall do my will, achieving the end for which I sent it" (Isaiah 55:11). Some among us are called to minister that word directly — to ensure that the faithful, as well as those who are not yet faith-filled, will continue to hear God's love spoken anew each time the sacred book is opened. These special people are called lectors.

At this point in the church's history, proclamation of the gospels — Matthew, Mark, Luke and John — is reserved to ordained clergy (deacons or priests). There is no compelling reason apart from custom and current legislation why the gospel should not be proclaimed by capable lay ministers. Ordination to the clerical state does not automatically bring effective proclamation skills; all that is demanded of the lector is likewise required of the gospel reader, for those who proclaim the gospels are likewise ministers of the word. They are faced with the same challenge and have the same purpose: to ensure that God's word will achieve the end for which it was sent. In response to their proclamation and clarion call, "The Gospel of the Lord," we cry out, "Praise to you, Lord Jesus Christ." Our response is our acknowledgment that God's word is alive with power. In our response we recognize its power to do what it says.

Each time the eucharist is celebrated, we hear Jesus say, "Do this in memory of me." At Mass we are doing something — not talking about something, not simply remembering something, not merely speaking words. We are speaking *deeds* — deeds that are accomplished at the moment they are spoken. God's word is an event, a happening, an accomplishment, a fulfilled promise, an act of love. And at its fullest expression, God's word is a person — Jesus, the Word made flesh. So it is with the proclamation of the word. It is far more than a telling, a relating, a recounting; it is God's Word becoming flesh in our midst in order to achieve the purpose for which it was sent — to redeem us in love. Can there be any more compelling reason to proclaim the word effectively?

Proclaiming a Word that Will Rouse Them

"The Lord has given me a well-trained tongue, that I may speak to the weary a word that will rouse them" (Isaiah 50:4). Those who refer to lectors or readers as "proclaimers" are making the very good point that there is more to the ministry of lector than simply reading the scriptures aloud in liturgical assembly. To rouse the weary, the word must indeed be proclaimed. That is, it must be uttered with conviction, clarity and skill. And God's word, as we have seen, is far more than words. It is, by its very nature, a proclamation—an announcement, a decree, a trumpet call summoning us to hear the great news that we are loved. Clearly, the proclaimer's ministry is a very special kind of reading.

And it requires special skills. The greater part of this guide outlines those skills, skills that are necessary for every kind of effective public reading. First, however, we need to make a distinction between reading aloud in public and proclaiming the word of God in the midst of the assembly on Sunday morning. The distinction is simple: Reading aloud in public has the purpose of informing, persuading or entertaining the hearers. While proclamation of the word can do all these things as well, it's central purpose is to celebrate and refresh the faith of the hearers.

After all, for church-going Christians there is no new information in Luke's gospel story of the birth of Jesus. They have heard it many times over. It is proclaimed each year to assembled worshipers to celebrate and refresh their faith in the God who loved them so much that he sent his only begotten son. It is precisely because they have heard it before that they want to hear it again. The challenge for the reader is to proclaim it in such a way that it is "heard again for the first time." That is, the story and the reality of our redemption is not simply a historical fact. It is an eternal act of love on God's part. It never ends.

In a mysterious way, the story of God becoming human in Jesus happens over and over each time we hear it and believe it. If the lector were to read the story with the idea that it is a tired old story everybody knows, it would probably sound like a tired old story that everybody knows. But if the story is proclaimed as an account of God's never-ending love affair with the human race, it will have a very different effect. Proclamation goes far beyond informing, persuading or entertaining. Effective proclamation rouses the weary, challenging them with its faith-filled conviction to hear and celebrate the good news again — for the first time.

The Proclaimer's Ministry in Salvation History

Jewish-Christian Tradition

This *Guide for Lectors* is part of a series of guides for a variety of ministries in the contemporary church. The series is evidence of an exciting new development, namely, the re-emergence of lay ministry, the participation of the laity in the day-to-day life and worship of the church. This is not so much a change as a return to the earliest Christian practice found in the New Testament. In the flush of the resurrection, the apostles set out to spread the story of Jesus to the farthest reaches of the world as they knew it. Soon, communities of Christians were springing up and establishing themselves, even in the face of persecution, as forces to be reckoned with.

The earliest Christians, we must remember, were Jews, members of that chosen race which had a long and rich association with the God whom Jesus came to reveal in a new way. Thus their worship was firmly rooted in the traditions and rituals of the Jewish synagogue and temple. Within that culture, the sacred word held an important place, both as an oral tradition and as the sacred books containing the accounts of God's intervention in the life of Israel. Readings from the sacred books were part of early Jewish and Christian worship.

Gradually, of course, the early Christians collected sacred writings inspired by the life and ministry of Jesus. In short, we have always been a "people of the book"; that is, the transmission of the good news has always been associated with a sacred text. Thus, there has always been something like the ministry of lector, specializing in the proclamation of the word of God as set down by the patriarchs, prophets, evangelists and apostles.

The Early Church

Ministry in the early church was loosely defined and arose in response to the needs of the people and the demands of a given community. But it is clear that there were different ministerial roles in the early church. Paul says as much when he teaches the Corinthians about the unity and diversity that characterize the church as the body of Christ:

> Now you are Christ's body, and individually parts of it. Some people God has designated in the church to be, first, apostles; second, prophets; third, teachers; then, mighty deeds; then gifts of healing, assistance, administration, and varieties of tongues. Are all apostles? Are all prophets? Are all teachers?

Do all work mighty deeds? Do all have gifts of healing? Do all speak in tongues? Do all interpret? (1 Corinthians 12:27–31)

It wasn't long before such a charismatic approach to ministry began to fade and a more hierarchical, more clearly defined and organized view of ministerial office replaced it. The result, as it would have been seen from within the Christian community, was a move away from spontaneous ministry — arising from need and exercising itself within the church — to a structured society of two levels, clerical and lay: those who ministered and those who were ministered to, so to speak. The clergy gradually assumed the responsibility and function of ministries that were originally performed by lay men and women. The current practice of reserving the proclamation of the gospel to ordained clergy may be seen in part as a remnant of that assumption.

Even a quick glance at church history shows that the distinction between clergy and laity grew more and more sharp over time, accounting in part for the many divisions that have splintered Christians over the centuries. Those who asserted the priesthood of Christ as shared by every baptized Christian rightly rebelled against a structure that seemed to reserve ministry to those officially ordained to it.

After Vatican II

Though it took a long time, the Catholic Church renewed its original view of church as a community of faith from which ministry arises according to need and individual God-given gifts. The Second Vatican Council confirmed this view, leading to the recent development of lay ministry, of which the ministry of lector is a part.

The ministry of lector or reader is new only in the sense that it is once again a lay ministry rather than a clerical one. Other lay ministries, more or less "officially" recognized, include those of the acolyte (altar server), minister of communion, church musician, catechist (teacher of religion), sacristan, bread maker, psalmist or cantor, lay preacher, and usher, among others. Clearly, we are again seeing the development of ministries according to the needs of the Christian community.

It is important that we see these lay ministries as true ministry — not simply duties carried out by generous laypersons eager to assist the clergy. It will no doubt be some time before this realization is clear, and if parish and diocesan communities continue to treat such ministers as "helping hands," the longer it will be. In the case of the lector, it is still common to see untrained and unskilled readers at the lectern — volunteers who have generous spirits but lack the formation and education necessary to proclaim the word of God in a compelling way.

We should not be surprised at this. The phenomenon of the lay minister is relatively new in the contemporary church. Though specific programs of formation (three to six months) and certain restrictions (minimum age 18) have been promulgated by the American bishops regarding lectors and acolytes, they are rarely heeded. The day may not be far off, however, when worshiping communities themselves will demand higher quality in the ministers who serve them. Those lectors who are of outstanding ability will be called upon to serve more regularly, and those who are in need of training will be given it. Others will find that they lack the necessary skills, time or dedication to serve as lectors. Once again, effective ministry within the church will arise in answer to a genuine need.

The church has provided ceremonies for the recognition and installation of well-trained lay ministers. One senses, however, that they are rarely celebrated, thus depriving the worshiping community of the realization that those who serve them do so as ministers prepared and equipped for service. On the other hand, it would be a mistake to call lectors to such institution ceremonies indiscriminately, simply for the sake of recognition. The ceremonial installation of lay ministers presumes and declares that they have been adequately trained.

This present *Guide for Lectors* is no more than an introduction to the ministry. It provides basic instruction for those who are without benefit of the thorough formation this ministry requires and deserves. But perhaps it will spur current and future lectors to demand full-fledged formation programs. If so, it will have more than served its purpose.

THE PROCLAIMER'S PROCLAMATION SKILLS

Preparation Skills

Experienced lectors and gospel readers gradually find methods of preparation that suit them best, so there is no intent here to legislate what is the right way — or even the best way — to prepare for the ministry of proclamation. It is important, however, for readers to remain open to new methods and to new resources so that their ministry will continue to deepen and grow.

"O Lord, open my lips and my mouth shall proclaim your praise." It is easy to forget, amid the work of honing communication skills and studying, that we are in the service of the Lord when we serve our fellow Christians through proclamation. Without maintaining and nourishing our own relationship with the Word made flesh, we can hardly expect to be genuine ministers of the words of scripture — where that incarnate Word is revealed.

The study of sacred scripture, whether for personal devotion or in preparation for proclamation, makes prayer an almost spontaneous response. But it is possible for the spontaneity to wane after some time, and our involvement with the word of God can take on the characteristics of purely scientific research. There's nothing wrong with bringing the very best of scientific technique to our study — indeed, the better equipped we are for knowing the cultural, linguistic and historical milieus in which the scriptures were written, the better chance we have of discovering the fullest intentions of the authors. God inspires human instruments to reveal the divine plan, and they respond, as we do, through the filter of their own experience.

The sacred scriptures have proved for many to be the springboard to a new and richer form of prayer. For one who is called to be a minister of the word, this would seem inevitable. The reader who has included prayer in the process of preparing a text is sure to bring the power, conviction and sensitivity of that prayer to the proclamation of it.

Abundant study resources are available to readers today and are well within the ability of the average person to understand. The challenge is not in finding the resources but in committing oneself to the time and effort required for intelligent and sensitive proclamation. We can no longer be satisfied with a simple reading of the words — we have all had the experience of a reader trying to deal with a text that he or she does not understand. The assembled worshipers cannot be aided in their celebration of faith when this occurs.

Sacred scripture can be read with profit even without study-ing it. But the scriptures are certainly more complex and far richer than many seem to realize. While the ministry of reader does not require a scholar's understanding of the Bible or of biblical criti-cism, you will certainly want to learn as much as you can about the sacred texts you proclaim. One who would be a minister of the word must be committed to the kind of long-term, concen-trated study that opens the scriptures ever more widely. And the commitment must be motivated by a profound sense of mission and service.

The value and profit of a group approach to praying and studying the scriptures can hardly be overestimated. Those who gather on a regular basis to examine the texts of the Bible are invariably better prepared to proclaim it or to hear it proclaimed to their benefit. How could it be otherwise? Christ is revealed in the scriptures. Saint Jerome put it this way: "Those who are igno-rant of the scriptures are ignorant of Christ." In faith communities where there is an energetic and committed scripture study group, those who proclaim the scriptures should be a part of it. It is not uncommon for lectors to band together and form their own group (or several groups), knowing that their spiritual welfare as well as their ministry will profit from such involvement.

Immediate preparation involves practice sessions — that is, reading the word aloud just as it will be read at the lectern, full voice and all. And we all need ongoing evaluation of our procla-mation and communication skills. At the very least, we should allow ourselves to be critiqued by a trusted friend or family member who will be honest and objective. Even better, those who serve as ministers of the word should gather from time to time and prac-tice as a group, providing mutual feedback and encouragement.

A certain breadth of view must characterize such sessions. Not all readers will sound alike — each person brings a separate and distinct charism to this ministry. On the other hand, the group should establish very clearly and early on that hypersensi-tivity to criticism must be surrendered. Good ministry is best eval-uated by those who are served, not by those who serve.

How Does One Prepare to Proclaim?

It may be helpful to demonstrate how to prepare for proclaiming the reading. Readers will, over time, develop preparation techniques of their own, but it is important, in any case, that your preparation be thorough and consistent.

Always begin with prayer. Since you are entering the realm of the inspired word of God, a brief prayer of praise and thanksgiving will enable you to begin your task in a spirit of openness, humility and gratitude. Scripture itself provides the best prayer, as a glance at the psalms, for example, makes clear.

After beginning with prayer, open the lectionary and read through all the texts (including the responsorial psalm and the Alleluia verse) assigned for the day on which you are to proclaim. It is important to get a sense of the dominant themes of a given Sunday. The reading you will proclaim is not isolated but is part of the texture of the whole celebration. Here, for example, are the lectionary texts for the First Sunday of Advent in Year A:

First Reading: Isaiah 2:1–5

The word that Isaiah son of Amoz saw
concerning Judah and Jerusalem.

In days to come
the mountain of the LORD's house
shall be established as the highest of the mountains,
and shall be raised above the hills;
all the nations shall stream to it.

Many peoples shall come and say,
"Come, let us go up to the mountain of the LORD,
to the house of the God of Jacob;
that he may teach us his ways
and that we may walk in his paths."

For out of Zion shall go forth instruction,
and the word of the LORD from Jerusalem.
He shall judge between the nations,
and shall arbitrate for many peoples;

they shall beat their swords into plowshares,
and their spears into pruning hooks;
nation shall not lift up sword against nation,
neither shall they learn war any more.

O house of Jacob,
come, let us walk in the light of the LORD!

Responsorial Psalm: Psalm 122

I was glad when they said to me,
"Let us go to the house of the LORD!"
Our feet are standing within your gates, O Jerusalem.

Jerusalem — built as a city that is bound firmly together.
To it the tribes go up, the tribes of the LORD,
as was decreed for Israel,
to give thanks to the name of the LORD.
For there the thrones for judgment were set up,
the thrones of the house of David.

Pray for the peace of Jerusalem:
"May they prosper who love you.
Peace be within your walls,
and security within your towers."

For the sake of my relatives and friends
I will say, "Peace be within you."
For the sake of the house of the LORD our God,
I will seek your good.

Second Reading: Romans 13:11 – 14

Brothers and sisters,
You know what time it is,
how it is now the moment for you to wake from sleep.
For salvation is nearer to us now
than when we became believers;
the night is far gone, the day is near.
Let us then lay aside the works of darkness
and put on the armor of light;

let us live honorably as in the day,
not in reveling and drunkenness,
not in debauchery and licentiousness,
not in quarreling and jealousy.

Instead, put on the Lord Jesus Christ,
and make no provision for the flesh, to gratify its desires.

Alleluia and Verse: Psalm 85:8

Alleluia.
Lord, let us see your kindness, and grant us your salvation.
Alleluia.

Gospel Reading: Matthew 24:37 – 44

Jesus spoke to his disciples:

"As the days of Noah were,
so will be the coming of the Son of Man.
For as in those days before the flood
they were eating and drinking,
marrying and giving in marriage,
until the day Noah entered the ark,
and they knew nothing until the flood came
and swept them all away,
so too will be the coming of the Son of Man.
Then two will be in the field;
one will be taken and one will be left.
Two women will be grinding meal together;
one will be taken and one will be left.

Keep awake therefore,
for you do not know on what day your Lord is coming.
But understand this:
if the owner of the house had known
in what part of the night the thief was coming,
he would have stayed awake
and would not have let his house be broken into.

Therefore you also must be ready,
for the Son of Man is coming at an unexpected hour."

Notice how closely related the readings are. The season of
Advent determines the choice of texts and their central concerns:
promise of the coming kingdom of peace, joy in the fulfillment of
the Lord's promises, optimism and the need to be prepared. The
unity of theme and purpose among all the texts makes each one
all the more rich.

The following commentaries are from an earlier edition of
the *Workbook for Lectors and Gospel Readers* (Year A). The *Workbook* is the best resource available today for the lector. It has been
published annually by Liturgy Training Publications for many
years. It contains brief, non-academic examinations of the readings with a twofold purpose: first, to extract the intellectual, emo-
tional and aesthetic content of the text, and second, to suggest
how the reader can effectively communicate that content, taking
into account the liturgical situation, the season and so forth. A
similar twofold purpose should guide your study and preparation,
regardless of the resource material you employ to assist you.

Commentary on Reading I: Isaiah 2:1–5

A new liturgical season begins today. But it does not startle us,
because the readings for the last few Sundays have already introduced the central idea: the last days, the "end of the world," the
completion of God's plan to bring all creation to perfection and
unity in divine love. All the images of "death, judgment, heaven
and hell" (what theologians have called the "four last things")
have been introduced in the final Sundays in Ordinary Time. The
new season of Advent puts these four last things into the context
of the coming of Christ — since it is with the birth of Jesus that
the kingdom of God on earth becomes present most vividly.

But the great plan of God to restore the world in perfect love
began long before Jesus, and the prophets of Israel saw visions of
this restoration process many centuries earlier. The prophet Isaiah
is a case in point. And it is very clear that the world he describes

in this first reading will be different from the present (his and ours). And the difference will be that all people will recognize God's law of love as the only way to universal peace.

You want to hasten these "days to come" as you read the first scripture passage of this new year of grace. Optimism and joy are always a part of new beginnings, and your voice can communicate encouragement, hope and new resolutions to the assembly in front of you.

The most compelling image here is the picture of nations reshaping their weapons of destruction into farm implements — tools for planting, growing and harvesting. Read this classic image in such a way that the assembly will hear it fresh — perhaps for the first time!

Special notes:

1. Amos is pronounced AY-muhz.

2. The people speak in response to the vision ("Come, let us go up to the mountain . . ."). A pause and renewed vocal energy is effective. The literary technique Isaiah uses in this poem (and remember as you read it that it is a poem) is parallelism. Almost every line has its parallel in the line that follows. (Example: For out of Zion shall go forth instruction, and the word of the LORD from Jerusalem.) Let the second line in each case be an echo of the first.

3. After the people speak, we return to the narrative of the vision.

4. The plea "Come . . ." is fervent, an invitation to renewal during the Advent season, when we prepare for the coming of the Lord in new ways.

Commentary on the Second Reading: Romans 13:11 – 14

Night and day. Darkness and light. Evil and good. Paul tells us in these images that dawn is approaching (the "light of the Lord" in the first reading). Thus the time associated with the darkness

of sin must give way to the time associated with the brightness of love.

The urgency of Paul's words fits the urgency of Advent. The word is out: God is moving toward us; we've got to move toward God. And that, of course, means moving away from less noble things.

In images of night and day, Paul even reminds us of the way we dress: Nightgowns and pajamas are not sturdy enough for the work we do during the day. We have to put on warmer and more protective clothing: "the armor of light" and "the Lord Jesus Christ." And once we are clothed in the Lord Jesus, we are equipped for good works.

Paul likes the notion of wearing our faith like armor. He tells us in his first letter to the Thessalonians (5:8) that this armor is made up of faith, hope and charity. You now invite the assembly to don the Christian uniform.

Special Notes:

1. These are words of comfort and encouragement. Be sure that they don't sound like a reprimand or threat.

2. Sentences that begin "Let us . . ." are most effective when spoken with great energy and conviction.

3. After a series of "nots," the reading ends with a strong contrast.

Commentary on the Gospel Reading: Matthew 24:37 – 44

The word "Advent," as you know, means "coming" or "arrival." We hear this idea in all three readings today: "In days to come," "the day draws near," and "the Son of Man is coming." We see again that Advent looks back in order to look forward. Jesus does precisely this in reminding us of Noah's time and the flood. And the purpose for looking back is that we may see ahead more clearly.

In a private session with his chosen twelve, Jesus explains at length what the end of time will be like. Today's reading is only a brief section of Jesus' discourse on the "parousia" — the coming of Christ in glory at the end of time. And the emphasis is on readiness, on being prepared.

It is very easy to get caught up in the flow of day-to-day activities and to become forgetful of the truly important things in life. It happened in Noah's time and it happens in ours. Jesus is not counseling us to live in fear and dread; rather, people are to live in expectation and hope, alert to the signs of God's loving plan to draw the world together.

You cannot avoid a sense of warning as you read this passage to the assembly, but the emphasis is really quite positive: We can profit from the lessons of the past. We know what it means to stay awake and not get caught off guard. It means being ready for the many ways God's love enters our lives — now, in subtle and humble ways (as in the birth of Jesus, which we will celebrate soon) and in more dramatic ways (as at the end of time — either our death or the end of the world).

It is not difficult for any of us to appreciate the value of a good "security system." So Jesus' final words in this reading make his point very clear. And, obviously, a good alarm system lessens our dread and makes us feel more secure, more prepared. The best alarm system for the Christian is a life lived in peaceful expectancy.

Special Notes:

1. Jesus, like the good teacher he is, explains with the use of historical example (Noah).

2. The example is applied ("So will it be . . .").

3. The final sentence is not so much a warning as a statement of fact.

No single method of preparation will be effective for everyone. Each lector will find his or her own favorite resource material and will discover the most effective way to prepare for proclamation. What the individual reader brings to his or her study will make it unique. And that is how it should be. No single mode of proclamation is prescribed for readers for the same reason.

Public Speaking Skills

The minister of the word at liturgical celebrations is competing for the attention of a culture awash in a sea of voices and images (television, movies, radio, the internet). Most of these voices are professionally bent on persuading us in some way (to buy something, to believe something, to behave in a certain way). While respecting the unique purpose of liturgical proclamation (communal celebration of faith), modern ministers of the word must develop a very high degree of skill in order to gain credibility with their audiences. People who hear professional speakers through the media every day — and who are in control of on/off buttons and volume controls — are naturally more demanding in their expectations of any speaker or reader who presumes to command their attention. *All the communication skills relevant to public speaking are relevant to liturgical proclamation.* This is not to say that the purposes of public speaking and liturgical proclamation are identical. They are not. The purpose of liturgical proclamation (and all liturgy) is ritual celebration of faith. It is not to inform, to persuade or to entertain (though it may do all three). But the *skills* required for effective proclamation are the same ones that we expect from public speakers, who are recognized for their ability to communicate effectively.

We know from personal experience that human speech can heal, destroy, provoke to anger or soothe the anguished heart. We have used it to express love, hate, disgust, ecstasy, anger and joy. We have heard others speak and have known that it can affect us quite profoundly, for good or ill. As readers we need to be profoundly aware of our power. Our proclamation of the word is never without an effect. The poorest proclamation, the mediocre proclamation, the most compelling proclamation — each affects the hearers in some way.

Yes, human speech is powerful. When employed in the proclamation of the word of God, it has a sacramental character: It is an exterior sign of an interior reality. Readers who thus see the power and responsibility entrusted to them will not take their ministry lightly.

Vocal Variety

Communication specialists tell us that the single most important quality of the public speaking voice is vocal variety. What audiences find most difficult to listen to is the monotone voice that lacks color, variations in pitch, animation and warmth.

Vocal variety is an umbrella term that includes all the characteristics of effective speech: rate, pause, volume, projection, and so forth. Each term is elusive and imprecise. What is "too fast"? How loud is "too loud"? When does a pause become "dead space"? In our discussion of vocal variety, keep in mind that the complexities of human speech sounds do not categorize very precisely. Matters of taste, individual preference and many other considerations

make the aesthetics of speech a very imprecise science. Nevertheless, we can certainly speak of what is effective and pleasant and generally considered "listenable." And we can certainly identify undesirable characteristics: monotonous, dull, inaudible, unclear, artificial or "phony."

The following passages require quite a lot of vocal modulation to communicate the various levels of meaning and an appropriate range of feelings. Don't be afraid to exaggerate vocal range when you are practicing — realizing, of course, that in actual proclamation such exaggeration would be out of the question.

1 John 5:5 – 6

[Notice that this passage contains a rhetorical question and that contrasts are involved ("not with water *only* but with water and the *blood*").]

Who is it that conquers the world but the one who believes
that Jesus is the Son of God? This is the one who came by water
and blood, Jesus Christ, not with the water only but with the
water and the blood. And the Spirit is the one that testifies, for
the Spirit is the truth.

Hebrews 11:1 – 9

[Note: The word *faith* has been italicized to indicate that it is the
recurring theme; a well-modulated and varied delivery will make
the word fresh each time — not as though it is a new idea each
time but the same idea with another aspect. By the time you pronounce the word for the last couple of times, it should feel and
sound like "an old friend."]

Now *faith* is the assurance of things hoped for,
the conviction of things not seen.
Indeed, by *faith* our ancestors received approval.

By *faith* we understand that the worlds were prepared by
the word of God, so that what is seen was made from
things that are not visible.

By *faith* Abel offered to God a more acceptable sacrifice
than Cain's. Through this he received approval as
righteous, God himself giving approval to his gifts; he died,
but through his *faith* he still speaks.

By faith Enoch was taken
so that he did not experience death;
and "he was not found, because God had taken him."
For it was attested before he was taken away
that "he had pleased God."

And without *faith* it is impossible to please God,
for whoever would approach him must believe that he exists
and that he rewards those who seek him.

By *faith* Noah, warned by God about events as yet unseen,
respected the warning and built an ark to save his household;
by this he condemned the world and became an heir
to the righteousness that is in accordance with *faith*.

By *faith* Abraham obeyed
when he was called
to set out
for a place that he was to receive as an inheritance;
and he set out, not knowing where he was going.

By *faith* he stayed for a time
in the land he had been promised,
as in a foreign land, living in tents, as did Isaac and Jacob,
who were heirs with him of the same promise.

Melody

Melody is a word associated with music, of course, and is perhaps the best term to use in discussing one aspect of vocal variation. It is also a risky word, because it may tend to make us think of "sing-song" when applied to speech. But melody in music refers to the movement of the pitch from one level to another — the kind of movement that must also typify the voice of the reader. When melody and lyric are complementary, as they are in the work of any good composer, each serves to augment and enhance the other. Nothing less is required in reading aloud.

Here is a particularly beautiful text from Paul's First Letter to the Corinthians. It is a hymn to love. The challenge for the reader is to treat it like the quasi-musical text that it is without sounding ridiculous or affected. Experiment broadly in your reading of this text. Consider even making up a simple tune to sing it by. Discover new ways to make each characteristic of love (patient, kind, not envious) stand on its own. The text demands a lot of "vocal music," and yet the music must not obscure the meaning.

1 Corinthians 13:3 – 14

If I give away all my possessions,
and if I hand over my body so that I may boast,
but do not have love, I gain nothing.

Love is patient; love is kind;
love is not envious or boastful or arrogant or rude.

It does not insist on its own way;
it is not irritable or resentful;
it does not rejoice in wrongdoing,
but rejoices in the truth.
It bears all things, believes all things,
hopes all things, endures all things.
Love never ends.

But as for prophecies, they will come to an end;
as for tongues, they will cease;
as for knowledge, it will come to an end.
For we know only in part, and we prophesy only in part;
but when the complete comes,
the partial will come to an end.

When I was a child, I spoke like a child,
I thought like a child, I reasoned like a child;
when I became an adult, I put an end to childish ways.
For now we see in a mirror, dimly,
but then we will see face to face.
Now I know only in part;
then I will know fully, even as I have been fully known.

Now faith, hope, and love abide, these three;
and the greatest of these is love.

By way of contrast, read the following passage aloud, noting the difference between it and the previous passage in terms of the degree and kind of melody required.

Acts 2:42 – 47

They devoted themselves
to the apostles' teaching and fellowship,
to the breaking of bread and the prayers.

Awe came upon everyone,
because many wonders and signs were being done
by the apostles.

All who believed were together and had all things in common;
they would sell their possessions and goods

and distribute the proceeds to all, as any had need.
Day by day, as they spent much time together in the temple,
they broke bread at home
and ate their food with glad and generous hearts,
praising God and having the goodwill of all the people.
And day by day the Lord added to their number
those who were being saved.

Clearly, some texts require a great deal more melody than
others. However, there is melody in every text. The difference is
determined largely by the difference in the kind of prose we're
dealing with. Paul's "hymn to love" is clearly poetic. The passage
from Acts is clearly narrative. Melody is determined by such
factors as topic, mood, purpose and literary genre (poetry, prose,
narrative, argument). Generally, the more exalted the subject
matter, the broader the melody patterns. But excesses are easy
to spot, and a degree of restraint and objectivity must always

characterize ritual proclamation. Your purpose is to proclaim the text, not to re-create or dramatize it. Above all, it is the *sense* and *feeling* of the passage that must guide you in all matters pertaining to effective communication.

Rate

The concept of "rate" involves more than a consideration of how fast or slow something is. Like "melody," the term "rate" can also be associated with a musical term: rhythm. So when we speak of how quickly or how slowly the reader reads, we are considering more than how long it takes to get from the first word of the passage to the last. Music teaches us rather quickly (almost intuitively) that rhythm is interesting when it is varied and not particularly interesting when it lapses into a steady beat without variation.

Consider a literary device employed throughout many books of the Hebrew scriptures: parallelism. It is a way of writing wherein each statement is echoed, or paralleled or expanded upon, in the next. Here is a classic example, in which the text has been spaced to illustrate the parallelism:

Joel 2:1 – 10

> Blow the trumpet in Zion;
> sound the alarm on my holy mountain!
> Let all the inhabitants of the land tremble,
> for the day of the LORD is coming, it is near —
> a day of darkness and gloom,
> a day of clouds and thick darkness!
>
> Like blackness spread upon the mountains
> a great and powerful army comes;
> their like has never been from of old,
> nor will be again after them in ages to come.
>
> Fire devours in front of them,
> and behind them a flame burns.
> Before them the land is like the garden of Eden,

> but after them a desolate wilderness,
>   and nothing escapes them.
>
> They have the appearance of horses,
>   and like war-horses they charge.

Read the text aloud, keeping in mind that each indented line echoes or expands upon the one before it. They share a parallel thought or image. The rate at which any such passage should be proclaimed is largely determined by its structure. Each pair of lines is separated from the others in a way different from the lesser separation within the pair. Although the rhythm may be constant, or at least patterned, the reading will be varied by other vocal elements: melody, pause, and so forth, all dictated by the varied meaning and feeling of each set of parallel texts.

And what about those very brief readings that almost seem over before they begin? Rate is definitely important in these cases.

How quickly? How slowly?
Some texts deserve a slower proclamation simply because they are dense in meaning or syntax, others because they are particularly solemn — or particularly brief. A very brief reading must be proclaimed slowly, lest it be over before the hearers have even become focused on it. Still other readings can profit from a degree of briskness. Consider the following:

2 Corinthians 13:11–13

[Note: This is the second reading on the Feast of the Holy Trinity (Year A). It is one of the briefest in the entire lectionary. It should take between 40 and 45 seconds to proclaim effectively, including the opening announcement and concluding dialogue. Time yourself.]

> A Reading from the second letter of Paul to the Corinthians.
>
> Finally, brothers and sisters, farewell.
> Put things in order, listen to my appeal,
> agree with one another, live in peace;
> and the God of love and peace will be with you.

Greet one another with a holy kiss.
All the saints greet you.

The grace of the Lord Jesus Christ, the love of God,
and the communion of the Holy Spirit be with all of you.

The word of the Lord.

Pausing

The challenge in effective pausing is learning not to fear silence. Many readers, especially those who are novices in the ministry, are afraid of the "sound of silence" when they are at the lectern. A steady stream of sound gives them the impression that they are moving along nicely and not stumbling over starts and stops. Unfortunately, the "steady stream of sound" is not pleasant for the hearers and can do violence to the text. Remember that your audience must process the text and is relying on your vocal presentation to endow the text with meaning, to signal changes in topic, to prepare them for a particularly significant part of the reading, and so forth. Effective pausing gives them time to do their processing. It also gives you time to refresh your understanding and your voice. Finally, a well-executed pause is one way of emphasizing a part of a text, either what has just been proclaimed or what is coming next. This is referred to as the "pause for effect."

Consider the following reading from the Acts of the Apostles on the Fifth Sunday of Easter (Year B). Here is an instance where we might distinguish three kinds of pauses, each signaling something different.

Acts 9:26–31

When Saul had come to Jerusalem,
he attempted to join the disciples;
[Slight pause: for effect]
and they were all *afraid* of him,
for they did not *believe* that he was a *disciple*.
But Barnabas took him,

brought him to the apostles,
and described for them how on the road he had seen the Lord,
who had spoken to him,
and how in Damascus he had spoken boldly in the name of Jesus.

So he went in and out among them in Jerusalem,
speaking boldly in the name of the Lord.

[Longer pause: new, but related topic]

He spoke and argued with the Hellenists;
but they were attempting to kill him.
When the believers learned of it,
they brought him down to Caesarea
and sent him off to Tarsus.

[Significant pause: completely new topic]

Meanwhile the church throughout Judea, Galilee,
and Samaria
had peace and was built up.
Living in the fear of the Lord
and in the comfort of the Holy Spirit,
it increased in numbers.

How long is a "brief" pause, a "significant pause," and so on? The subtlety of the spoken word makes it inadvisable (even impossible) to apply anything like a mathematical value to vocal elements (count to one, count to three) or even to use arbitrary markings (/ = brief pause; // = medium pause; /// = long pause). Any such system is subject to individual or idiosyncratic interpretation. Demonstration by a seasoned and well-received reader can help, but is not always available. The best guarantee that you will employ pauses (and all elements of vocal variety) effectively is three-fold: (1) your sensitivity to spoken language and how it works; (2) your thorough understanding of the text; and (3) your courageous desire to share it fully with your audience.

Volume: How Loud?

Contemporary audiences will not tolerate insufficient volume, because ordinarily, they do not have to. In informal conversation they ask their communication partner to speak up. Radios, TV's and other sound media have volume controls. If your reading is simply not loud enough, then something else will be perceived as louder. And that something else could be crying infants, the air-conditioning system, a restless congregation or the "inner noise" that we all have playing in our heads at every moment. If something is louder (let alone more interesting and commanding of attention), the reading will not be heard.

But sheer volume is not the answer. Excessive volume is even more disagreeable than insufficient volume. Just as important as sound level is sound "height" and "weight," or pitch and projection. Depending on the environment in which your ministry is exercised (cathedral or chapel), the "height," or pitch, of the voice must be elevated accordingly. And the voice must take on a proportionate degree of "weight," or projection strength, as well.

Let's say you are sitting on the back porch with your neighbor, engaged in conversation, watching your young children play on the swing set in the backyard. How would your voice sound as you and your neighbor swapped stories? Now you notice that Robby is pushing Mark's swing too high, so you call out, "Not so high, Rob!" How does your voice sound now? It's not only louder, it's higher (pitch) and weightier (projection). This situation is not so different from any public communication situation to which your voice must adapt. Sheer volume (loudness) is not sufficient. Otherwise, the volume control on the public address system could solve the problem. Imagine how your quiet conversation with your neighbor would sound booming through a microphone system. A little ridiculous, to say the least. And yet, there seem to be many readers/speakers who think they can speak in a normal conversational tone at the lectern because the microphone will do all the work. For liturgical readers, it helps to recall that our ministry is called "proclamation."

The following text may be good for practicing sufficient projection. It was obviously proclaimed energetically in its original setting. There should be no sense that you are re-enacting the original situation, of course, but the tone of your voice should echo the "weight" of the occasion and the text itself. The exultation in the voice of the prophet Zephaniah calls something more from the reader than a storyteller's tone. Imagine how inappropriate (almost laughable) these words would sound if they were muttered quietly or without expression. But notice too that the mood changes in the second paragraph. A sensitive reader would not read the two paragraphs alike. Experiment broadly with this text, and don't be afraid to exaggerate as you practice. Nothing even approaching exaggeration should appear in your proclamation of it, of course, but the voice and the body "remember" the energy of an exaggerated rehearsal and retain it.

Zephaniah 3:14–18

> Sing aloud, O daughter Zion;
> shout, O Israel!
> Rejoice and exult with all your heart,
> O daughter Jerusalem!
> The LORD has taken away the judgments against you,
> he has turned away your enemies.
> The king of Israel, the LORD, is in your midst;
> you shall fear disaster no more.
>
> On that day it shall be said to Jerusalem:
> Do not fear, O Zion;
> do not let your hands grow weak.
> The LORD, your God, is in your midst,
> a warrior who gives victory;
> he will rejoice over you with gladness,
> he will renew you in his love;
> he will exult over you with loud singing
> as on a day of festival.

Consider, by way of contrast, this gentle text from Isaiah. A favorite of many, it begins with a quiet (but still heard!) opening, moves through an exultant passage and then moves on to an exhortation, concluding with a strong assertion of confidence.

Isaiah 40:1–11

[Question: How do you begin this reading gently and yet ensure that it will be heard by all? Answer: Pause for a significant amount of time after announcing the reading, looking at the assembly. Silence can sometimes command attention very effectively.]

> Comfort, O comfort my people, says your God.
> Speak tenderly to Jerusalem, and cry to her
> that she has served her term, that her penalty is paid,
> that she has received from the LORD's hand
> double for all her sins.

[Obvious elevation of volume here:]

> A voice cries out:
> "In the wilderness prepare the way of the LORD,
> make straight in the desert a highway for our God.
> Every valley shall be lifted up,
> and every mountain and hill be made low;
> the uneven ground shall become level,
> and the rough places a plain.
> Then the glory of the LORD shall be revealed,
> and all people shall see it together,
> for the mouth of the LORD has spoken."

[And perhaps another here:]

> A voice says, "Cry out!"
> And I said, "What shall I cry?"
> All people are grass,
> their constancy is like the flower of the field.

[Sudden slight decrease in volume here?]

> The grass withers, the flower fades,
> when the breath of the LORD blows upon it;
> surely the people are grass.
> The grass withers, the flower fades;
> but the word of our God will stand forever.

[Clearly, something new is required here:]

> Get you up to a high mountain,
> O Zion, herald of good tidings;

> lift up your voice with strength,
> O Jerusalem, herald of good tidings,
> lift it up, do not fear;
> say to the cities of Judah,
> "Here is your God!"

[Quiet strength? Bold affirmation?]

> See, the Lord GOD comes with might, and his arm rules for him;
> his reward is with him, and his recompense before him.
> He will feed his flock like a shepherd;
> he will gather the lambs in his arms,
> and carry them in his bosom,
> and gently lead the mother sheep.

The appropriate volume for this passage will not be the same throughout. But be careful: Even the most tender words must be heard clearly by the worshiper farthest from you, and the exhortation should not blast those sitting nearby. Variances in volume in liturgical proclamation are subtle but nonetheless effective. Remember too that all the elements of vocal variety work together. A rise in volume is usually accompanied by a rise in pitch, a higher energy level, more forceful projection, a slightly slower or faster pace, and so forth.

Public Speaking Anxiety: Stage Fright

Whether you are experienced or new at this ministry, you should be dealing with the number one phobia in nearly every human being: public communication anxiety — or, in more popular terms, "stage fright." If you do not experience this anxiety at all, chances are you are not taking your ministry seriously enough — or have settled for "safe" methods that render your reading too "casual," too low-key, lifeless and ineffective.

That rather stern remark brings us to the first step in dealing with stage fright: It has a positive side. Remind yourself that such anxiety is the fear of not doing a good job — or the fear of looking ridiculous. The positive side is that your fear is really the energetic desire to do well.

There is no cure for public speaking anxiety. And there is no wish to "cure" it. Rather, the constructive approach is to "use" it — to use the energy underlying it. The best way to use that energy is to prepare well and then proclaim the word with a high energy level. All the experts in the field of communication agree that thorough preparation is the best way to address stage fright.

In addition, you can control the physical evidence of stage fright by breathing deeply and slowly and by becoming familiar with the liturgical environment — and even enhancing it (a suitable lectern, a lectionary book that is worthy of its function, an adequate public address system, and so forth). Public performance is a skill and an art. Practice not only makes perfect (or nearly so), it also creates confidence. Therefore, seek every opportunity for public speaking experience, so that your success rate is elevated. Finally, remind yourself that you share the challenge of stage fright with every dedicated performer, preacher and reader.

Proclamation Skills

While effective communication skills are universal — that is, they are required for every public speaking situation, including proclamation of the word — there are adaptations that need to be made according to the variables of audience expectation, occasion, communicative purpose, environment, and so on. Liturgical proclamation requires sensitivity to the special nature and unique elements of the liturgical setting.

The ministry of reader presumes the context of an assembled worshiping community, and sacred scripture (as arranged in the lectionary for use throughout the liturgical year) is the reader's medium. Though readers are often called upon, in less than ideal circumstances, to deal with other texts (the responsorial psalm, general intercessions, announcements), the ministry of proclamation is for the purpose of proclaiming the scripture readings and the ritual dialogues that introduce and conclude them. Our considerations henceforth presume that the effective communication

skills desirable in any human exchange are seen in the particular context of ritual and worship.

Ritual Language

The nature of ritual language is that it is more formative than informative. Ritual language, like liturgy itself, is concerned with "doing" more than "telling." In the proclamation of the word of God, the action of God intervening in human history is continued. The words we proclaim achieve their purpose and are fulfilled in the very proclamation and hearing of them. It is necessary to insist on the special nature of ritual language in order to avoid a more pragmatic view of proclamation that would see it as instruction, information, persuasion or anything other than gratuitous praise and the continuation of God's will to redeem us in love.

Consider this: After you have been a minister of the word for several years, you will be dealing over and over again with familiar texts. Certainly your adult hearers are witnessing the proclamation of texts that they have heard over and over all their lives. Ritual language is not concerned with hearing something *new*. It is concerned with expressing the familiar and hearing it *anew* each time the ritual is celebrated. The minister of the word is not a teacher, not a channel of information, not a persuader. Beginning readers especially have a difficult time redefining themselves as ritual proclaimers and not information bearers.

Read the following passage, a very familiar one, and ask yourself why it is heard over and over and over again. There is no new information here; there is no moral instruction; there is no effort to directly persuade the hearers in any way. Why repeat it over and over? If you come up with a practical and pragmatic answer, you will miss the point. If your answer employs such terms as memorial, tradition, heritage and so forth, you are edging up on a good response. If you decide that the passage is repeated because the story it tells is fulfilled in the telling of it, and the inauguration of the kingdom of God is not limited to time or space, you will proclaim it in accord with its ritual purpose.

Luke 2:1 – 14

In those days a decree went out from Emperor Augustus
that all the world should be registered.
This was the first registration
and was taken while Quirinius was governor of Syria.
All went to their own towns to be registered.
Joseph also went from the town of Nazareth in Galilee to Judea,
to the city of David called Bethlehem,
because he was descended from the house and family of David.
He went to be registered with Mary,
to whom he was engaged and who was expecting a child.

While they were there,
the time came for her to deliver her child.
And she gave birth to her firstborn son

and wrapped him in bands of cloth,
and laid him in a manger,
because there was no place for them in the inn.

In that region there were shepherds living in the fields,
keeping watch over their flock by night.
Then an angel of the Lord stood before them,
and the glory of the Lord shone around them,
and they were terrified.
But the angel said to them,
"Do not be afraid; for see —
I am bringing you good news of great joy for all the people:
to you is born this day in the city of David a Savior,
who is the Messiah, the Lord.
This will be a sign for you:
you will find a child wrapped in bands of cloth
and lying in a manger."

And suddenly there was with the angel
a multitude of the heavenly host,
praising God and saying,
"Glory to God in the highest heaven,
and on earth peace among those whom he favors!"

Now consider this text (the First Reading on the Feast of All Saints), which is filled with rather extraordinary images and information. It takes the qualities of ritual language to new heights. The reader should approach texts such as these for what they are: exalted and poetic attempts to express the ineffable. They do not survive well under the weight of a staid rendition devoid of passion. [The bracketed portion of the text has been omitted from the lectionary. The ritual numbering of each tribe seemed too much for the average hearer. For our purposes here, it is included because it is an exceptional example of the semi-hypnotic power of ritual language.]

Revelation 7:2 – 14

I, John, saw another angel ascending from the rising of the sun,
having the seal of the living God,

and he called with a loud voice to the four angels
who had been given power to damage earth and sea, saying,
"Do not damage the earth or the sea or the trees,
until we have marked the servants of our God
with a seal on their foreheads."

And I heard the number of those who were sealed,
one hundred forty-four thousand,
sealed out of every tribe of the people of Israel:
[From the tribe of Judah twelve thousand sealed,
from the tribe of Reuben twelve thousand,
from the tribe of Gad twelve thousand,
from the tribe of Asher twelve thousand,
from the tribe of Naphtali twelve thousand,
from the tribe of Manasseh twelve thousand,
from the tribe of Simeon twelve thousand,
from the tribe of Levi twelve thousand,
from the tribe of Issachar twelve thousand,
from the tribe of Zebulun twelve thousand,
from the tribe of Joseph twelve thousand,
from the tribe of Benjamin twelve thousand sealed.]

After this I looked,
and there was a great multitude that no one could count,
from every nation,
from all tribes and peoples and languages,
standing before the throne and before the Lamb,
robed in white, with palm branches in their hands.
They cried out in a loud voice, saying,
"Salvation belongs to our God
who is seated on the throne,
and to the Lamb!"

And all the angels stood around the throne
and around the elders and the four living creatures,
and they fell on their faces before the throne
and worshiped God, singing,
"Amen! Blessing and glory and wisdom
and thanksgiving and honor and power and might
be to our God forever and ever! Amen."

Then one of the elders addressed me, saying,
"Who are these, robed in white,
and where have they come from?"
I said to him, "Sir, you are the one that knows."
Then he said to me,
"These are they who have come out of the great ordeal;
they have washed their robes
and made them white in the blood of the Lamb.

Liturgical Dialogue

"The word of the Lord." "Thanks be to God." "A reading from the holy gospel according to Luke." "The Gospel of the Lord." "Praise to you, Lord Jesus Christ." Liturgical dialogue is effective when the principle of "expected form" is observed. It loses its ritual power when it is departed from in the mistaken interest of making it literal, relevant, "warm" or informative. Thus it is important that readers be faithful to the dialogue assigned to them, not embellishing or augmenting it in any way. To do so is to destroy the appeal of liturgy and ritual as an expected form of worship. Ritual works its long-term and subtle effect on us precisely because of its repetition and predictability. The constant search for new and potentially disarming ways to alter liturgical dialogue reveals a woeful lack of understanding of liturgy's purpose and function.

In recent years, we have heard readers at pains to "refresh" liturgical dialogue by creating their own versions of it. "The word of the Lord" has seen such permutations as "And this, my brothers and sisters, is the word of the Lord." The content of the two statements is the same, perhaps, but the form, function and purpose are all radically different. Aside from the fact that the assembly will be caught off guard and not be able to respond with spontaneity, the casting of the dialogue in this literal and "informative" way misses the mark in two ways: It destroys the expectations with regard to "form," which are essential to ritual, and it "tells" us something instead of "does something."

Several years ago, the ritual form was officially changed by the church. You may recall that the reader used to say at the end of the reading, "This is the word of the Lord." The formula was reduced to "The word of the Lord," not only in the interest of a better translation of the Latin (*Verbum Domini*), as some have asserted, but to render it more ritual ("doing something") and less referential ("telling something"). "This is . . ." clearly carries a feeling of the demonstrative — explaining in part the tendency of some readers to hold the lectionary aloft as they spoke the words. This practice confused things further by drawing attention to the book when the proper focus of our attention should have been on the living proclamation of the word still ringing in our ears. The simple change from "This is the word of the Lord" to "The word of the Lord" has a subtle and important effect over time. It lessens our tendency to see the liturgy as a gathering in which we "learn" about our faith and intensifies our experience of the liturgy as a gathering in which we "celebrate" our faith.

Scriptural Language

All of sacred scripture is written in exalted language. This is because the scriptural writers were always engaged in communicating something more than just their actual words. Even what appears to be the most straightforward narrative has a deeper purpose. The deeper purpose explains, in part, why the gospel narratives of Matthew, Mark and Luke differ so much from one another. The writers had a governing purpose not only in recording events in the life of Jesus but in recording them *in a certain way*. And the Gospel of John is radically different from the synoptics. In John's account of the passion, for example, Jesus is very much in control of the situation. He is not victim; he is king and ruler. A loyal band of followers stands at the foot of his cross. In the other accounts, it is a mocking crowd. John's purpose is different, so he portrays the passion of Jesus differently. Such controlling themes elevate prose far beyond the merely literal and project it into the realm of the figurative, even the poetic.

The point is that casual attempts to "translate" the translation into colloquial, informal, or even "everyday" expressions are irresponsible, revealing a lack of understanding of scripture and the subtleties of its original form. More serious still is the effect of such attempts, no matter how well-intentioned or motivated: They invariably and inevitably trivialize sacred scripture. They also underestimate the sensitivities of the hearers and foreground the speaker at the expense of the word of God.

Biblical Literary Genres

The Bible is a collection of many different kinds of literature: narratives (stories), poetry, sermons, hymns, and so on. Your instincts will tell you that different kinds of literature require different treatments. Trust your instincts. But avoid stereotypes. There is no reason to imitate bad Shakespearean actors when reading poetry, or Mother Goose when reading a narrative.

There is a very important reason for recognizing and respecting the different literary styles in the Bible, and it has been alluded to above. The writer's message is told in a particular way (literary form) because the writer is making a particular point or appealing to the audience in a particular way. The choice of style is not arbitrary. A classic example, of course, is the poetry of Genesis and the accounts of creation. If we forget that the writer's purpose is to show that God is the origin and the sustaining power of all that exists, we could repeat the mistake of trying to understand the poetic text literally. Knowing that there are two accounts of creation in Genesis — which do not agree with each other — should be enough to convince us that the authors were not concerned with scientific data. Poetry is usually not the style of choice for scientists.

Readers who have studied literature during their high school and college years should not hesitate to approach the Bible as a collection of literature in a variety of genres. All that you studied regarding metaphor, simile, narrative, plot and denouement (resolution) is applicable. Poetic structure, word order, alliteration, onomatopoeia — these terms apply to biblical poetry and can be helpful. Yes, many poetic elements such as these are lost in translation, but the better translations today have been done by scholars who have tried to preserve them.

The point here is the same one emphasized throughout this book: Readers often bring to their ministry a wealth of experience that should be capitalized upon, not tossed aside in the mistaken notion that the literature of the Bible — and the successful proclamation of it — is so rarefied that it requires a whole new frame of reference.

Poetry

There is a great deal of poetry in the Bible. The Psalms, Proverbs, much of the Wisdom literature and long sections of the prophets all are written in poetic form. The challenge to the reader is to have the courage to read them as the poetry they are instead of like prose. For the most part, such adjustments in proclamation style will come naturally to the sensitive reader. There is no recommendation here to over-dramatize or become lugubrious in response to a poetic text. There is encouragement, however, to suggest the strong emotions and feelings that are so often found in poetry.

Narrative

The scripture reading below is in narrative form. We have dealt with this text before in the discussion on effective pausing. Notice that it is, in effect, a short story — the story of Saul's first difficulties in overcoming his reputation as a persecutor of the fledgling church and before he becomes "Paul, apostle to the Gentiles." Narrative can move between events and commentary on those events quite easily. That is what happens here. In the narratives of the gospels, and especially in the passion of Jesus, there is an even more straightforward telling of events but always an underlying tone or purpose. What is the purpose of recording the events in the reading below? Is it to record the change in how Saul/Paul is received? Is it to provide an opportunity for sharing the story of Saul's conversion ("he had seen the Lord")? Is it to remind the reader of the rejection suffered by the good news ("attempting to kill him")?

Yes, it is all these things, but the summary paragraph at the end is probably our best guide. The vicissitudes involved in spreading the good news cannot suppress it. The believers are growing in number and in strength. In every narrative there is usually a controlling idea or theme that explains its presence. Try to find that theme and formulate it in your own words. Thus your proclamation of the narrative will be more cohesive and intelligible, tying events together under the guiding theme.

Acts 9:26–31

> When Saul had come to Jerusalem,
> he attempted to join the disciples;
> and they were all afraid of him,
> for they did not believe that he was a disciple.
> But Barnabas took him,
> brought him to the apostles,
> and described for them how on the road he had seen the Lord,
> who had spoken to him,
> and how in Damascus he had spoken boldly in the name of Jesus.
>
> So Saul went in and out among them in Jerusalem,
> speaking boldly in the name of the Lord.
> He spoke and argued with the Hellenists;
> but they were attempting to kill him.
> When the believers learned of it,
> they brought him down to Caesarea and sent him off to Tarsus.
>
> Meanwhile the church throughout Judea, Galilee,
> and Samaria
> had peace and was built up.
> Living in the fear of the Lord
> and in the comfort of the Holy Spirit,
> it increased in numbers.

Discourse

In discourse, an argument is being presented, an explanation is being offered, or the writer is simply drawing out the implications

of an event or a divine action. Here Paul is explaining that
although our redemption has been accomplished in Christ, it is
not yet fully realized. It is what some have called the great irony of
Christian life, the "already, but not yet" experience. We've already
been saved, but we are still being saved, and the full experience of
our salvation lies in the future. Thus, the natural condition for
believers is one of hope.

Paul extends the longing for the fullness of salvation to the
earth itself, as all creation (even inanimate creation) is incom-
plete until the fullness of redemption and re-creation is complete.
The earth itself is "hoping" for that day of full restoration when
God and creation will be in perfect harmony — as in the days
before Adam's sin. That sin subjected everything to futility; Jesus'
death and resurrection liberated everything in hope!

Romans 8:18 – 23

I consider that the sufferings of this present time
are not worth comparing with the glory
about to be revealed to us.
For the creation waits with eager longing
for the revealing of the children of God;
for the creation was subjected to futility,
not of its own will
but by the will of the one who subjected it,
in hope that the creation itself
will be set free from its bondage to decay
and will obtain the freedom of the glory of the children of God.

We know that the whole creation
has been groaning in labor pains until now;
and not only the creation,
but we ourselves, who have the first fruits of the Spirit,
groan inwardly while we wait for adoption,
the redemption of our bodies.

Discourse is, in some ways, the most difficult literary genre to proclaim, and it is sometimes even more difficult to hear. It requires more study, a deeper analysis of prose structure, and a very careful rendering. Very often it is a theological kind of logic that is used in discourse — more typical of the Middle Eastern mentality than our own Western syllogistic kind of argumentation. The reader will have to surrender a tendency to grasp irritably for hard facts in biblical discourse. But the development of argument is cogent, given the writer's method and intention.

THE PROCLAIMER AND THE WORD

When you answer the call to be a minister of the word (one who proclaims the Bible readings to the assembled faith community), you enter a deeper relationship with the word of God as revealed in sacred scripture. You take upon yourself the duty and privilege of bringing the printed word to life — making it flesh, so to speak. Your ministry as reader gives voice to God's healing and strengthening word as it goes forth irrevocably to the ends of the earth, achieving the purpose for which God sent it. In a very real sense, you become a prophet — one who speaks for God. You become another John the Baptist, preparing the way of the Lord, making crooked paths straight and rough places plain. You take upon yourself the task and joy of delving ever deeper into the mystery of God's presence in the world through the revealed word.

You join yourself to an ancient tradition in Jewish life that sees no more worthy occupation than the study and service of God as experienced in the sacred texts. As a Christian you identify yourself with the age-old belief that God's words find their fullest expression in one perfect word: the Word made flesh, Jesus the Christ.

As you begin this new ministry, or as you seek to enhance a ministry you have performed for quite some time, recall frequently that the degree and kind of relationship you establish with the word is the wellspring of your service. As the relationship deepens, you will see yourself more and more as a disciple — one who is not merely taught but *formed* by the master. And it is precisely as a well-formed disciple that you will be most effective in revealing the face of the master to those whom you are called to serve.

The Minister

The reader proclaims the word to the assembled faith community. It's that simple and that sublime. The ministry is a simple one, though not in the sense that it's easy to do well or requires little energy or effort. Simplicity refers to the mode of the ministry, the reader's ability to proclaim the word transparently so that the word itself, and not the proclaimer, is in the foreground. Simplicity does not, however, refer to the reader's task — for the task itself is quite challenging. Not everyone is equal to it.

There is no wish here to contradict or to criticize any long-established local practice that is in accord with liturgical principles and directives. On the other hand, it is apparent that excessive enthusiasm has, in some communities, introduced practices into the liturgy that can only be called theatrical. Theater is a noble and powerful art form; there is no intention here to discredit it. But liturgy is not theater, even when its fullest expression is quite dramatic. The purposes of the two are profoundly different: theater, to create a vicarious experience for an audience; liturgy, to express and celebrate the immediate faith experience of all present.

Posture and Attitude (Nonverbal Language)

Members of the assembly know well that their experience of liturgical worship is affected by the manner in which the leaders of the liturgy conduct themselves. Excessive formality, bordering on coldness or arrogance, should be just as foreign to our expression of faith as its equally inappropriate opposite: excessive cordiality, bordering on false intimacy or sentimentality. Persons of good will and average sensitivity will know almost intuitively that the liturgy requires dignity and restraint, an alert reverence that communicates awareness of the significance of ritual worship. Individual readers may need to be reminded (or shown how) to present themselves, body and spirit, in such a way that the assembly they serve will be edified, not distracted.

Good, relaxed posture, neither stiff nor careless, is a must, not only because of the signal it gives but because it is required for effective use of the body in public communication. Experts in the field remind us over and over that "nonverbal language speaks loudest." Nonverbal language is everything but the words coming from your mouth (including "ah"s, "uh"s, body language, dress, posture, attitude, and so on). If the way we present ourselves to an audience is disagreeable or distracting, it will drown out anything we have to say. Readers who shift rhythmically from one foot to the other, lean into the microphone or wear enormous, dangling earrings have allowed unfair competition to accompany them to the lectern. Their nonverbal language will drown out their proclamation.

The words "dignity" and "restraint" may carry negative connotations for some readers, but they probably best describe the kind of decorum appropriate for ritual worship. "Mastery of the situation and task" is a phrase that should carry only positive connotations and describes the goal that readers should strive for most earnestly. Readers who "master" the functions of their ministry are accorded the kind of credibility that enables them to minister most effectively.

There is an element of the sublime in the work of the reader as well. To be chosen to proclaim God's word to one's fellow believers is to participate in the mystery and struggle of their individual journeys in faith. There can be no more sublime ministry than that. And there can be no more humbling responsibility — for the quality of the reader's proclamation determines whether his or her service will help or hinder the hearers.

Men and women who take on the ministry of reader are presumed to be of good faith, eager to serve their fellow Christians and willing to engage in ongoing formation into effective service. But it is not presumed that they are particularly holy, exceptionally gifted, or highly skilled in communication techniques. Basic abilities are required, and these have been the subject of part of this *Guide*. Highly developed communication skills related to certain professions (public speaking, broadcasting, acting, for example) must be developed by the reader, but they do not, in themselves, render a person capable of effective liturgical proclamation. The purpose of liturgical worship is very different from the objectives we find in the work of professional communicators: conveying information, entertaining, persuading to action, and so forth. The liturgy may do all of these things, of course, but they are not its purpose, which is to celebrate the faith shared by the worshipers.

Finally, the mere wish or willingness to serve as reader does not qualify one for the ministry. This statement sounds harsh; no one wants to discourage a volunteer. But the fact remains that the ministry of reader is a charism for the building up of the community. It requires certain native abilities that some do not have, such as an adequate vocal instrument, for example. It also requires self-possession and confidence, maturity, poise and sensitivity to diversity in one's audience. Such qualities can be enhanced in a formation program but should already be present to a significant degree in the potential reader.

Like all official ministries in the church, liturgical proclamation of the word is an awesome responsibility to which one is called and into which one is formed. Fifteen hundred years ago, Saint Benedict wrote in his *Rule:* "They should not presume to read who by mere chance take up the book. . . . Only those are to discharge these duties who can do so to the edification of the hearers."

The Word

When we hear the expression "the word of God," we intuitively, or perhaps because of our Judeo-Christian formation, realize that more is being referred to than a simple "word." The "word of God," we sense, means "all the words of God." Or perhaps it means "the Bible," and certainly for Christians it means Jesus Christ, "the Word made flesh," the "incarnate Word." The familiar liturgical dialogue that follows every reading, "The word of the Lord/Thanks be to God," has a formative influence on us over time. It creates in our hearts and minds an association between the words of the reading and the benevolent actions of the God who revealed them.

That association is even more vivid in the languages in which the texts we hold sacred were originally written. The Hebrew word for "word" is *dabar,* and it means "deed" (an action) as well as "word." In this definition, words are not merely sounds or symbols that describe deeds. Words are themselves deeds. Our tendency at this point might be to see such an association as "merely poetic." But "word as deed" is not a view found only in the highly intuitive thought of the Middle East, where our scriptures were born. Language scholars in the contemporary West have formulated a similar view. They demonstrate that words are not always just sounds or written symbols that *refer* to something, as in "There is the house where I live." In some usages, words actually *do* something. And in these cases they are called "performative speech acts." A simple example: The words "I baptize you" or "I forgive you" or "Bless you!" do not simply refer to an action; they actually accomplish the action they describe.

The point is that we understand the words of liturgical proclamation more accurately when we view them as "performative," as accomplishing the work of salvation they describe even as the reader proclaims them. The word of God is not a history lesson, though there is history in it. The word is not a story, though it is full of stories. It is not a set of rules to live by, though there is much in it to guide our choices. No, the word of God is a living and dynamic presence, achieving the very salvation about which it speaks even as the reader proclaims it. The church has taught us this view in the words, "Christ is present in his word since it is he himself who speaks when the holy scriptures are read in the church." And, again, "In the liturgy God speaks to his people and Christ is still proclaiming his gospel" (Vatican II, *The Constitution on the Liturgy*).

In the reader's proclamation, the word of God is alive with power, achieving the sanctification of the people to whom it is proclaimed and rendering glory to the very God whose creative word brought all things into being.

Conclusion

There is great cause for rejoicing in a church that is beginning to reap the fruits of many laborious years of renewal and change. One of the most significant changes in the liturgical lives of Catholic Christians has been a renewed emphasis on the Bible, the word of God. From a time, not very long ago, when Catholics had every right to be embarrassed about their ignorance of sacred scripture, we have come to an age when the word of God is once again proclaimed as a heritage we can proudly claim. From a time when study of the Bible was perceived as a heady occupation only for scholars, we have come to a day when informal study groups pursue biblical literature with courage and insight. From an age when the liturgy of the church exposed us to very few of the words of sacred scripture, we have arrived at a time when the liturgical proclamation of the word once again holds it rightful place. Our Sunday assemblies come together to break the word and to break the bread.

And with the resurgence of the word in our midst, it was only a matter of time before we would experience the need for ministers of that word, not just functionaries to pronounce the words aloud but true ministers called from among the people of God to become bearers of the word, lovers of the word, custodians of the word. Through their study, their prayer, their skills and their faith, they break open the word for us. We are nourished from the lectern as well as from the altar.

Let readers accept the challenge issued them by the church's need in our day. Let them become masters of their task, lovers of their calling. Let them be John the Baptist, a herald's voice, filling in the valleys and lowering the hills — making a straight path for the Lord in the hearts of all who have ears to hear.

Bibliography

Workbook for Lectors. Published annually by Liturgy Training Publications, *Workbook* includes all the readings for the Sundays and major feasts of the liturgical year, with commentaries, helpful markings in the text and suggestions for effective proclamation. Also published in Spanish under the title *Manual para procla-madores de la Palabra*.

A Well-Trained Tongue: Formation in the Ministry of Reader, by Aelred Rosser. A thorough treatment of the ministry of lector, complete with exercises and suggestions for establishing an ongoing reader formation program. Published by LTP.

Proclaiming the Word: Formation for Readers in the Liturgy, written and narrated by Aelred Rosser. A video program that examines the ministry of reader through the testimony of four seasoned lectors.

A Word That Will Rouse Them, by Aelred Rosser. Reflections on the ministry of lector and its development, practice and future. Published by LTP.

Lector Training Program: This Is the Word of the Lord, produced by Michael J. Sparough, SJ. Three audiocassettes containing twelve 15-minute lessons for lectors. Lessons include: the steps of preparation, volume and the microphone, pacing and pauses, eye communication, word stress and inflection. Includes a 27-page booklet for use with the tapes and a reproducible evaluation form.

Guide to the Revised Lectionary, by Martin Connell. An easy-to-understand book that answers common questions about the Roman Catholic lectionary: its origins and history, how scripture is organized, what is left out, and more. Clear and concise information for lectors, preachers and all members of the assembly. Published by LTP.

Pronunciation Guide for the Sunday Lectionary, by Susan E. Myers. A handy, inexpensive pocket guide for proclaimers of the Word, containing the words and names used in the readings for Sunday Mass and feast days. Published by LTP.

The Revised NAB Sunday Lectionary. Three 10 x 14 inch volumes, one for each year of the three-year lectionary cycle. Readings are arranged in sense lines for ease of proclamation. Cover art on each volume evokes the Tree of Life and the Cross and was created using five light-reflecting foils. Includes over forty pieces of original interior art. Each volume also contains a dedication page and a quality ribbon marker. Published by LTP.

Study Edition of the Sunday Lectionary. A convenient and comprehensive paperback volume containing the readings for Sundays and feast days, the complete Introduction to the lectionary, lists of readings and psalms, and several helpful charts and tables. Ideal for long-range planning of liturgies, homilies and music. Published by LTP.